AF477761

# Roaming the East Coast Route

ERIC TREACY

LONDON

IAN ALLAN LTD

By the same author:

Steam Up
Main Lines Across the Border (with O. S. Nock)
Lure of Steam
Portrait of Steam
Glory of Steam
Spell of Steam
Roaming the Northern Rails

First published 1977

ISBN 0 7110 0812 4



Published by Ian Allan Ltd Shepperton Surrey
and printed in the United Kingdom by
Ian Allan Printing Ltd

THE
ELIZABETHAN
60009
A4

## FOREWORD

Of railway books there seems to be no end. Photographers are digging into stocks of old negatives, in some cases, going back over a period of 50 years. To this, I am no exception. It is an exercise encouraged by the publishers who, presumably, have a good idea as to the demands of the railway addicted public. Each time I do this, I think that I have come to the end of my material – but always there is something left to be printed. The surprising thing is that there is some remarkably interesting material that has not been published.

In this book, there are a few pictures which the observant may spot as having been published previously, but there is a great deal of new material. As I have prepared these photographs my memory has ranged back over the apparatus that I have used. To this day, I use a Lancaster Enlarger which is over 40 years old. It creaks a bit, and is a heavy brute to move about, but it still gives good service. I have been through the whole spectrum of cameras – Soho $\frac{1}{4}$ plate Reflex, 9 x 12 Press Camera, Leica 35 mm, $2\frac{1}{4}$ sq Rolleiflex, 6 x 9 cm Super Ikonta, and various Japanese monsters! There are pictures in this book taken with all these cameras. Now, after nearly 50 years in the game, I have come back to my Super Ikonta and Rolleiflex. They are light to carry, simple to use, reliable in performance, and have lenses better than anything now being made by the modern camera makers.

I am sometimes asked how I obtain my results, and briefly my answer is (apart from merit!) : use a film and developer you know (in my case, TRI X and D76 at half strength) ; and don't listen to all the tales that enthusiasts tell you about the latest apparatus – photographic enthusiasts tend to be of all people the most gullible!

The railway photographer is a solemn bird, greeting his competitors with a suspicious eye. They tend to be selfish, sacrificing their wives and children to their hobby. As house pets they are intolerable, taking possession of the bathroom, staining the carpets, putting poisonous liquids in milk jugs. I wonder that anyone has anything to do with them! And yet, it may be said of them that they are socially harmless, they don't go about armed, they are usually sober, and the better operators give a good deal of pleasure to other people.

There are different types of railway photographers. First, there is the snapshotter, who bangs away at everything with an Instamatic, who sometimes snaps a train moving at 100mph at $\frac{1}{25}$th second, and to everybody's amazement but his own, often gets surprisingly good results. Next, there is the chap who does it at odd moments and tends to haunt the same location because he works near it. Then there is the chap who is totally dedicated. To whom money is no object. He can travel the world in his hunt for steam. He is here, there, and everywhere, perhaps with his own helicopter. He will have a gadget which enables him to take black and white, colour, and ciné at the same time. And then there is the chap who sets up his camera, bribes a small boy to keep an eye on it, and disappears into the nearest pub with a cable release about a mile long, and does it by remote control.

Where do I come in all this? I think that I am the sort of chap who enjoys railway photography very much, but I am not prepared for it to so master me that I am its slave. If you become too much addicted, it loses its pleasure and becomes something of an obsession, and you can't enjoy doing anything else. I am an old-stager now, I look back on 50 years of shooting steam, and I am very grateful for all it has brought me – friends, fresh air, the satisfaction of portraying a splendid machine in a variety of settings; and the entrée into the world of the railwayman, where there exists a high percentage of very nice people who, somewhat surprisingly, seem to appreciate the interest of a reasonably well-informed layman. To all such, my greetings, and thanks for services rendered.

Eric Treacy

Two Class 55 Deltics at their journey's end in Kings Cross.

# INTRODUCTION

Once upon a time the East Coast Route was a combined operation of the Great Northern Railway, the North Eastern Railway, and the North British Railway. Then this Trinity found unity in the London and North Eastern Railway. Now it is the joint responsibility of the Eastern and Scottish Regions of British Rail.

The East Coast Main Line, for the purposes of this book, starts at Kings Cross and ends at Edinburgh Waverley (if you are a Sassenach), and vice versa if you wear a kilt. As I am a Sassenach, with a touch of the Irish, I am starting at Kings Cross. Not the most handsome of stations, opened in 1852, designed by Lewis Cubitt: its two main sheds are enclosed by a brick facade crowned by a central clock tower. It is notable that this clock and its neighbour on the St Pancras clock tower are never in agreement as to the time of the day. It has been remarked that the frontage of Kings Cross station bear resemblance to a Cossack Riding School. As I have never seen a CRS, I wouldn't know if that were so, or not!

The same Cubitt designed the Great Northern Hotel adjacent to the station. This hotel is scarcely a jewel in the Crown of the British Transport Commission's Hotel Executive.

During the reign of the good King Richard (Marsh) considerable improvements were carried out at Kings Cross. The new Travel Centre at the south end of the station was opened and the booking office was transferred with Messrs W. H. Smith from the old Platform 10. This platform has now been re-numbered, but for the life of me I can't remember the new number. Suffice to say that at the end of this platform, for which platform tickets are not required, there congregates the usual motley crowd of spotters. The coming of diesels at first brought about a falling-off in the gallery, but numbers are up again as Deltics are hunted as keenly as A4s.

Credit where credit is due. BR have done their best with Kings Cross. They have improved it without destroying its character, as they did up the road at Euston, after a complete re-building.

During my time as Bishop of Wakefield I made many a journey to London on official business. Nearly always the same thing happened. Our Deltic made light work of its 8-coach train, arriving at Finsbury Park on time, or slightly before, and then the crawl started down the hill to Kings Cross, usually with a dead stop between the two tunnels. I guess that the reason was lack of platform availability in Kings Cross station.

I have always thought that the obvious thing was to combine St Pancras and Kings Cross stations, keeping one for arrivals, and the other for departures.

In the old days of steam there was a sense of excitement as the locomotive emerged tender-first from the Gas Works Tunnel on its way from the 'Top Shed'. What was going to take the 10 o'clock – an A4, A1, or an A3? There is no doubt as to the ceremony surrounding the arrival of a steam locomotive to take its train – the coupling up, the ritual on the footplate, the consultation with the guard; the moment of starting, the roar from the chimney, the hiss from the cylinder cocks. Slowly, the train disappears from view, leaving behind a trail of smoke and steam.

Certainly an event, of which the enthusiast never tired.

I recall occasions during the war when a train would consist of 20 carriages, packed with uniformed humanity. The engine, usually a filthy V2, would be hidden in the tunnel, confronted with a climb the moment it started. Once those massive trains got over the top at Potters Bar, they put up some magnificent performances with those huge loads.

Today, the Deltics walk up the hill, usually passing Finsbury Park in 4½ minutes. Of course, they are handling much lighter loads than the Pacifics. It was a daily occurrence for a steam engine to handle trains of 14 or 15 coaches weighing nearly 500 tons full. The fast Inter-City trains handled by the Deltics usually consist of 8 or 9 vehicles weighing about 330 tons. I should like to see how a Deltic would perform with 15 coaches behind it.

There is little enough on which to comment between Kings Cross and Peterborough. Indeed this is true of the East Coast Route until Selby, where the magnificent Abbey is to be seen to the west of the line. When the East Coast Route is diverted on account of the new Selby coalfield, travellers will be deprived of this magnificent view.

The modern Inter-Cities will make

Peterborough in 58 minutes. I have timed them at 50 minutes. No longer is speed reduced to 25mph as trains negotiate that dog leg through the old Peterborough Station. Now they nip through at 100mph, and are up and over Stoke Bank in 15 minutes and through Grantham, 105 miles from London, in 1 hour 10 minutes.

And so on to Doncaster. Little enough, so far, on which to feast your eyes. The traveller can read his paper, chat to his neighbour, go to the dining car, or sleep, safe in the knowledge that he is missing nothing worth seeing outside the train.

Gradually, there comes a change in atmosphere. The red brick of the south and the Midlands is giving way to the grey stone of the north. South of Doncaster there are spoil heaps and pit heads. There is scarcely a point from which it is not possible to see squadrons of cooling towers emitting their clouds of vapour.

Within two hours of leaving Kings Cross, your train either stops at Doncaster, or flashes through the station on the middle road. To the west, there is the 'Plant', the birth place of countless Great Northern engines, later of the Gresley, Thompson, and Peppercorn Pacifics.

And so to York – nothing much to trouble the engine here. The line runs through flat and uninteresting country. York is one of the most magnificent cities in Europe, but you don't see much of it from the train. The station is built outside the city walls, trains going north turn immediately west on leaving the station, so that the Minster is difficult to see.

The station is a magnificent piece of building, designed by Thomas Prosser, and opened in 1877. It is built on a curve and has an impressive roof. Its long platform is 500 yards from ramp to ramp. Northbound trains had to get moving on this curve, and in the days of steam there was some monumental slipping at this end of the station. Joy for tape recordists and photographers, but hell to the men on the footplate.

We cannot leave York without mention of George Hudson, the York draper, known as the Railway King. This tough Northerner became MP for Sunderland, and to his energy and initiative we owe many of the country's most important main line railways. In the year 1844, Hudson was in control of all the railways, built, or being built, between Rugby and the Tweed. Alas for poor George. Like so many ambitious speculators he overreached himself and he met financial disaster. But his works remained, and he was recently reinstated in public esteem when the Archbishop of York (Dr Coggan) named a street after him adjacent to the headquarters of the Eastern Region in York.

Now, this introduction must shorten its 'cut-off', and move to journey's end. We can dispense with a mile-upon-mile description of our northward journey. We have passed from Great Northern territory into the North Eastern marches. From York, we launch ourselves over the 45 miles of straight and level track to Darlington. To the East, the Cleveland Hills; to the West, the Pennines. We shall probably pass Darlington station on the 'down fast', which avoids the station.

Had we stopped in Darlington station you would have caught a glimpse of George Stephenson's *Locomotion* on its pedestal in the station. At least, you would have done a year ago. It has recently been removed to the Darlington North Road Railway Museum – which is, I think, a pity.

Soon we come to one of the most dramatic and impressive views in Europe. We approach Durham cautiously over the viaduct and to the east there opens up a view of Durham Cathedral and Castle. This is best seen in an autumn morning with a misty sun climbing up into the sky behind the Cathedral. Easy work follows down to Newcastle. The train crosses the Tyne over the King Edward VII Bridge. This bridge, opened in 1906, made it possible for trains to run through Newcastle without reversing, which had been the case when there was only Robert Stephenson's High Level Bridge.

Like York, Newcastle Central station is on a curve, but unlike York, it has a magnificent classical entrance. Should you alight from the train at Newcastle and fall into conversation with the natives, you might well think that you had fetched up in Scandinavia. In Yorkshire, you will be addressed as 'luv' by all and sundry: in Newcastle you will be 'hinnie'. Once you can understand them, you will find they are lovely people. I spent six months in these parts during the war, and you could not have found kinder hearts.

Actually, the old Newcastle Central station was a most photogenic place, producing wonderful effects of light and shade (see page 87).

Out of Newcastle, we are away to the Border for the last stage of our journey. On this leg of the journey, it really justifies the title East *Coast* Route, because once the line is north of Morpeth, the sea is never far away. Across Robert Stephenson's superb viaduct over the Tweed, with its 28 arches, 126ft above the river bed, to the right there is a glimpse of the estuary with the North Sea beyond; to the left as you come off the bridge, the ruins of Berwick Castle. Now we pass from North Eastern territory to that which was originally North British.

Contrary to a generally held belief, Berwick-upon-Tweed is not the border: this is at Marshall's Meadows about three miles north of Berwick. And a singularly un-impressive border it is, tucked away in a cutting below a caravan site. Now there follows an enchanting stretch of line with glimpses of the blue sea and the border hills. Through Penmanshiel tunnel, the train tears down the bank at Cockburnspath, skirts the lush Lammermuirs, and across the Firth of Forth, visibility permitting, you will glimpse the Kingdom of Fife.

And so we approach the end of this 393 mile journey from Kings Cross. On the non-stop 'Scotsman' in the days of steam, engine crews had changed by means of the corridor tender at Tollerton nine miles north of York, but not so the engine which might well have hauled 500 tons of train nearly 400 miles. It was for this kind of hard labour that Gresley designed his magnificent series of Pacifics.

There are those who hold that the intrusion of Waverley Station and its approach lines into the heart of Edinburgh is monstrous vandalism. I can understand their feelings as I look out over the undulating sea of glass from Princes Street. But then, I am biased, as are countless others who hold Waverley station in affection. It possesses one feature that none will dispute. The steps from the station up to Princes Street are the draughtiest known to man. Crowning it all is the aggressively ugly North British Hotel, but in a curious way, its ugliness is impressive. Its clock tower and the Scott Memorial, viewed dispassionately, are hideous, but they have so established themselves as part of the Edinburgh sky-scape that their demolition would be unthinkable, and opposed strongly by the descendants of the environmentalists who protested about their being put there in the first place.

The great thing about Waverley station is that it is *in* Edinburgh, and you come straight out of the station into the City. Although it is a through station, it manages to give the impression of journey's end. If you have come non-stop from London you certainly realise that you are 400 miles nearer the North Pole than where you started your journey. There are few more biting winds than the 'har' – an east wind straight off the Firth.

So, we come to journey's end for the East Coast Route. When the 'Non-stops' were introduced in 1928, the journey took $8\frac{1}{4}$ hours. In 1932, things were speeded up and the journey time reduced to $7\frac{1}{2}$ hours. Later the A4s 'non-stopped' in 6 hours and now the Deltics draw into platform 10 in 5 hours 27 minutes. From London, the most heartless and ruthless city in Britain, they have traversed the flat Fens, threaded the South Yorkshire coalfield, crept through York 'without the walls', dashed across the Plain of York, saluted the burial place of St Cuthbert in Durham Cathedral, crossed the Tyne and the Tweed, come over the Border and ended in that city which never fails to exert its magic over the visitor.

This book offers a pictorial record of this journey: a tribute to the engines which have pounded up the East Coast Route, and to the men, from Kings Cross, Grantham, Doncaster, York, Newcastle and Haymarket who have driven them and delivered so many thousands of travellers safely to their journey's end.

*Above left:* Not, as it would appear, a train double-headed by two Pacifics – I suppose it has happened on the East Coast Route, but I have never seen it. These two Pacifics, coupled together, had come down to the station from the Top Shed. Immediately after this photograph was taken the A4 (No 60025 *Falcon*) uncoupled from the A3 (No 60103 *Flying Scotsman*) and made off for other duties.

*Left:* Although this picture has appeared before in one of my books, I include it again because it so admirably expresses the aggressiveness, not only of these powerful engines, but of Ted Hailstone the driver. I have rarely seen an engine burst out of Kings Cross as No 60014 *Silver Link* does in this picture with the down 'Tees-Tyne Pullman'.

*Above:* A4 No 60006 *Sir Ralph Wedgwood* at Kings Cross with an afternoon train for Leeds.

If I dare to say that Kings Cross has more to offer the enthusiast than any other of the great London termini, I suppose that I shall be in trouble with those who dote on Paddington: or there may even be some who would put Euston top of the league.

Kings Cross has been modernised but it has not lost its original character. Mercifully, some of the draughts at the South end of the station have been dealt with. One of the remedies for this are doors that remain shut until the passenger is within a few feet of them, when by means of some gadget I don't understand, the door automatically opens for him and shuts behind him. These doors are fascinating to children who pass many a happy hour operating this self-opening machinery, in the course of which they are a perfect nuisance to everybody.

No station in London offers the facilities which are to be enjoyed at the end of the old Platform 10.* From here, the station saunterers can watch the departures and arrivals, as well as having a good view of the goings on in the locomotive yard. Then, if you have a permit, and don't mind getting dirty, you can take up your position above the tunnel mouth with a superb view of what is happening in the station. That was where I was standing when I took this photograph (*below*) of the down 'Flying Scotsman' leaving the 'Cross' for Edinburgh behind A1 Pacific No 60156 *Great Central.*

I was standing half way up the steps of the signal box (now demolished) to photograph A4 Pacific No 60007 *Sir Nigel Gresley* leaving for Yorkshire with the down 'Yorkshire Pullman' (*right*).

*This was written early in 1977 before the alterations to the layout at Kings Cross.

YORKSHIRE
PULLMAN

A
B
C
D
1N06

1A14
0C01
1A30

Morning and evening at Kings Cross – the old and the new in Motive Power. It is 9.20 am by the clock on the tower of St Pancras station as Class 55 Deltic No 9012 *Crepello* leaves K ngs Cross with a train for the West Riding of Yorkshire. How much better the Deltics looked when they were painted dark green with the lime green band over the wheels (*above left*). It is 5.30 pm when A4 Pacific No 60014 *Silver Link* heads north on a beautiful summer's evening with the down 'Yorkshire Pullman' (*above*).

*Left:* What is the collective noun? A 'nestle' of Diesels, perhaps. Whatever it is, here are a lot of them in the locomotive yard at Kings Cross.

During Mr Peter Townend's time as Locomotive Shed Master at Kings Cross, the main line engines were a joy to behold. Whenever you encountered an engine with the 34A shed plate, it would be immaculate. I would recommend Mr Townend's book *Top Shed* as quite one of the best railway books ever written. How splendid that the Shed Master was also a superb photographer!

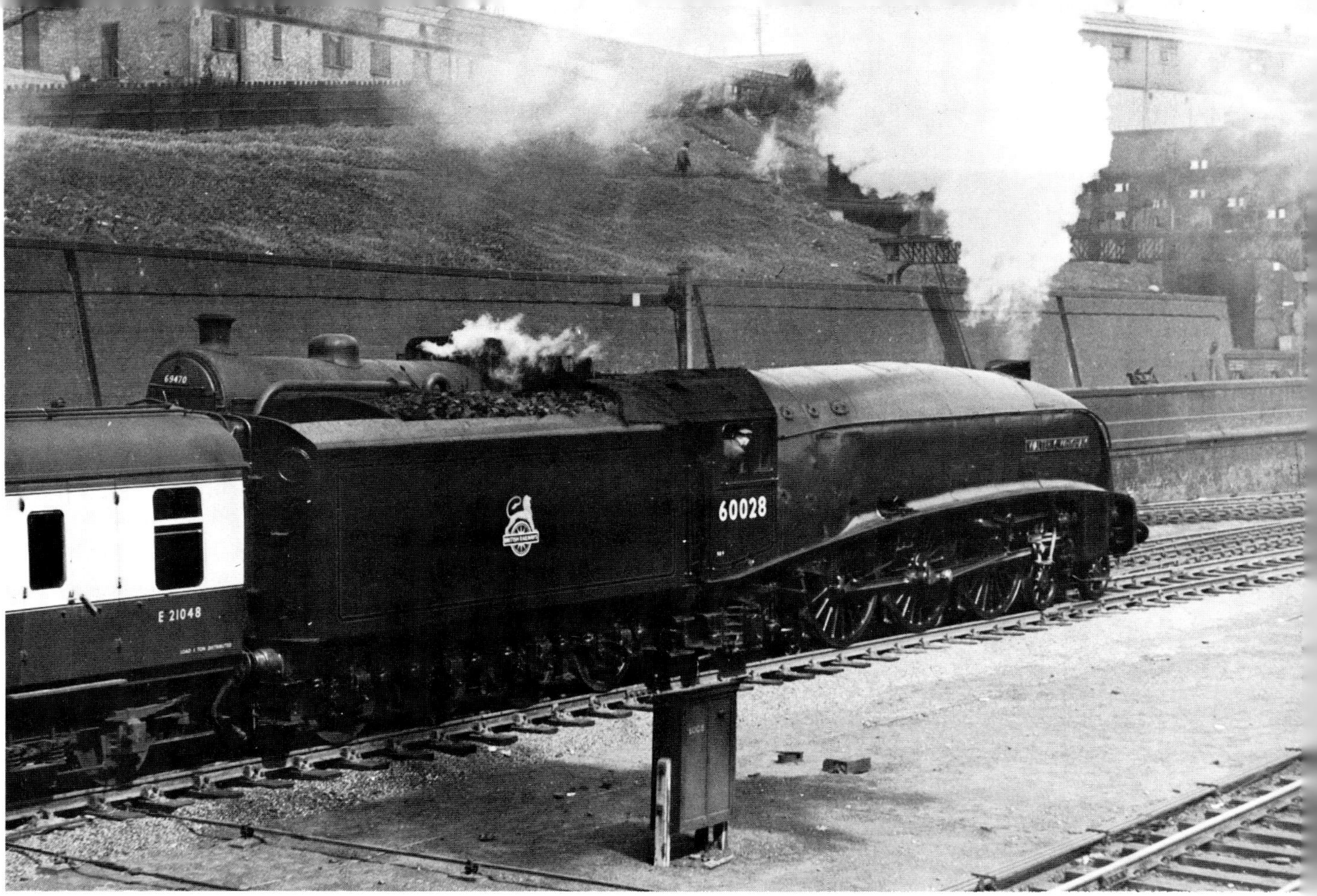
69470
60028
E 21048

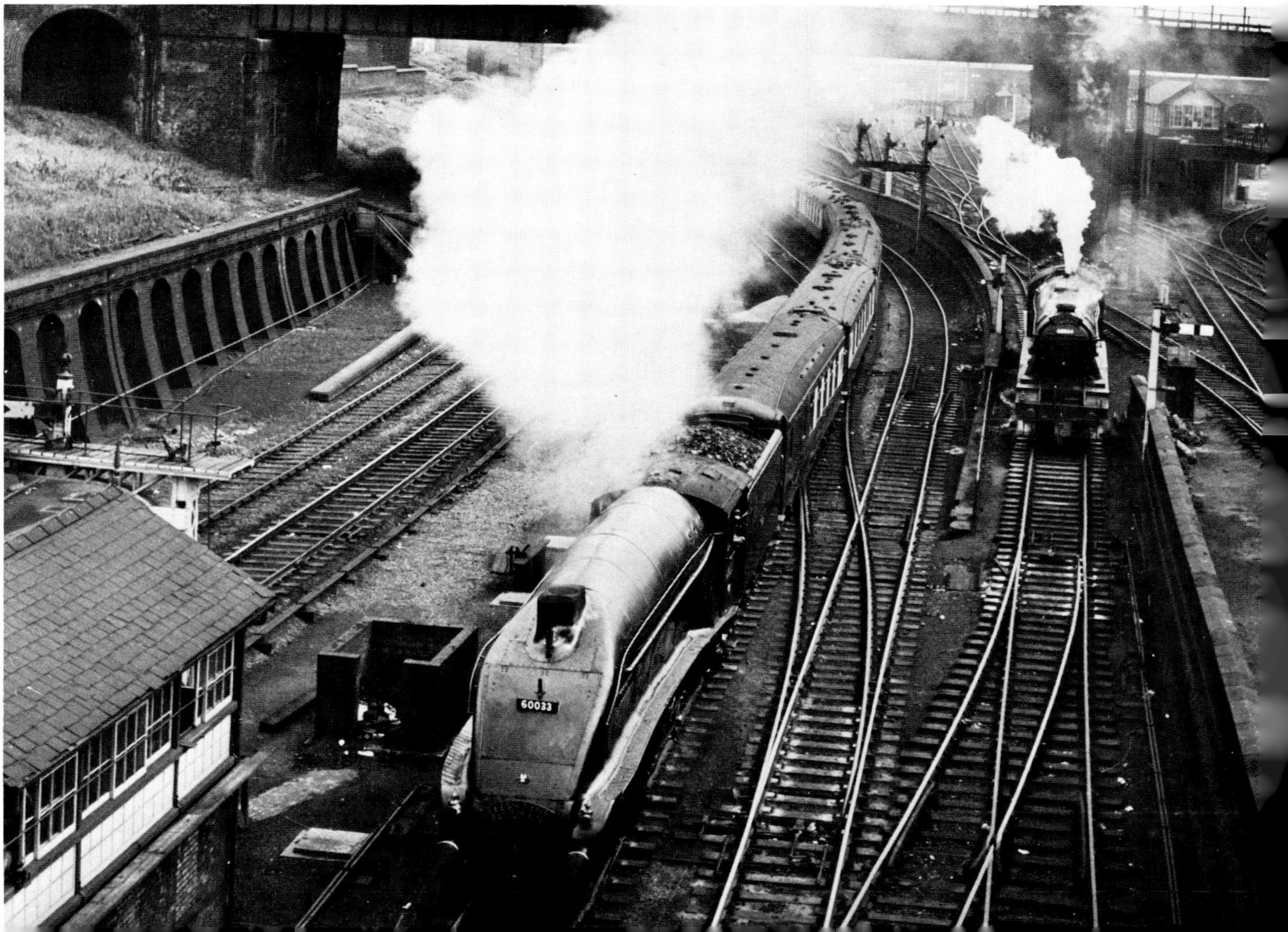
60033

There are two tunnels within a mile of the platform end at Kings Cross – first the Gas Works Tunnel, then the Copenhagen Tunnel. Between the tunnels has been a happy hunting ground for photographers, but no more, as Eastern Region have withdrawn lineside photographic facilities. Disappointing as this is for many people, it is a step that was inevitable in view of the speeding up of trains, and the dangers of having foreign bodies lurking around the tracks. On the whole, British Rail have been very kind to lineside photographers, and I, for one, would want to say how much their permits have been appreciated.

Here we are with three shots between the Tunnels.

*Above left:* A4 Pacific No 60028 *Walter K. Whigham* heads for Copenhagen Tunnel with train for Bradford and Leeds.

*Left:* The 'Tees-Tyne Pullman' passes Copenhagen Box. A4 Pacific No 60033 *Seagull.*

*Above:* Class 55 Deltic No 9018 *Ballymoss* passes Belle Isle Box heading a train for the West Riding.

'Between the Tunnels', once you can get there – and it's not easy – northbound traffic is slogging up the hill; engines from Top Shed are queuing up to get to the station; and most inward traffic is halted at the signals – so there's always a lot to see.

Here we have (*below*) the non-stop 'Elizabethan' behind A4 Pacific No 60028 *Walter K. Whigham.*

*Right:* a grubby A3 No 60102 *Sir Frederick Banbury* climbs the bank with a train for Peterborough while A3 No 60061 *Pretty Polly* waits to go down to the station to take out the 'Yorkshire Pullman'.

*Below right:* Brush Type 47 No 1512 brings the 'Master Cutler' to the capital from Sheffield.

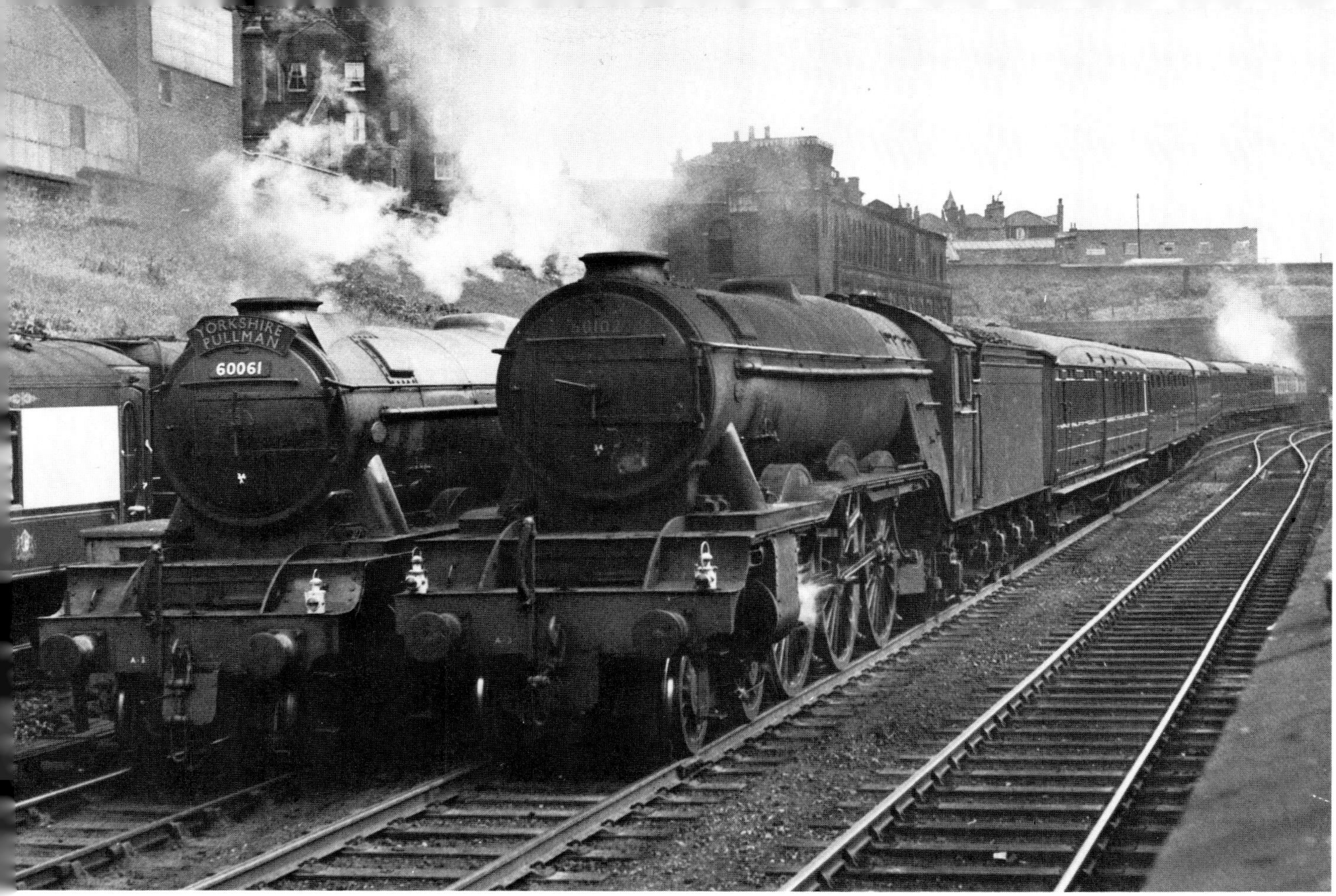
YORKSHIRE PULLMAN
60061

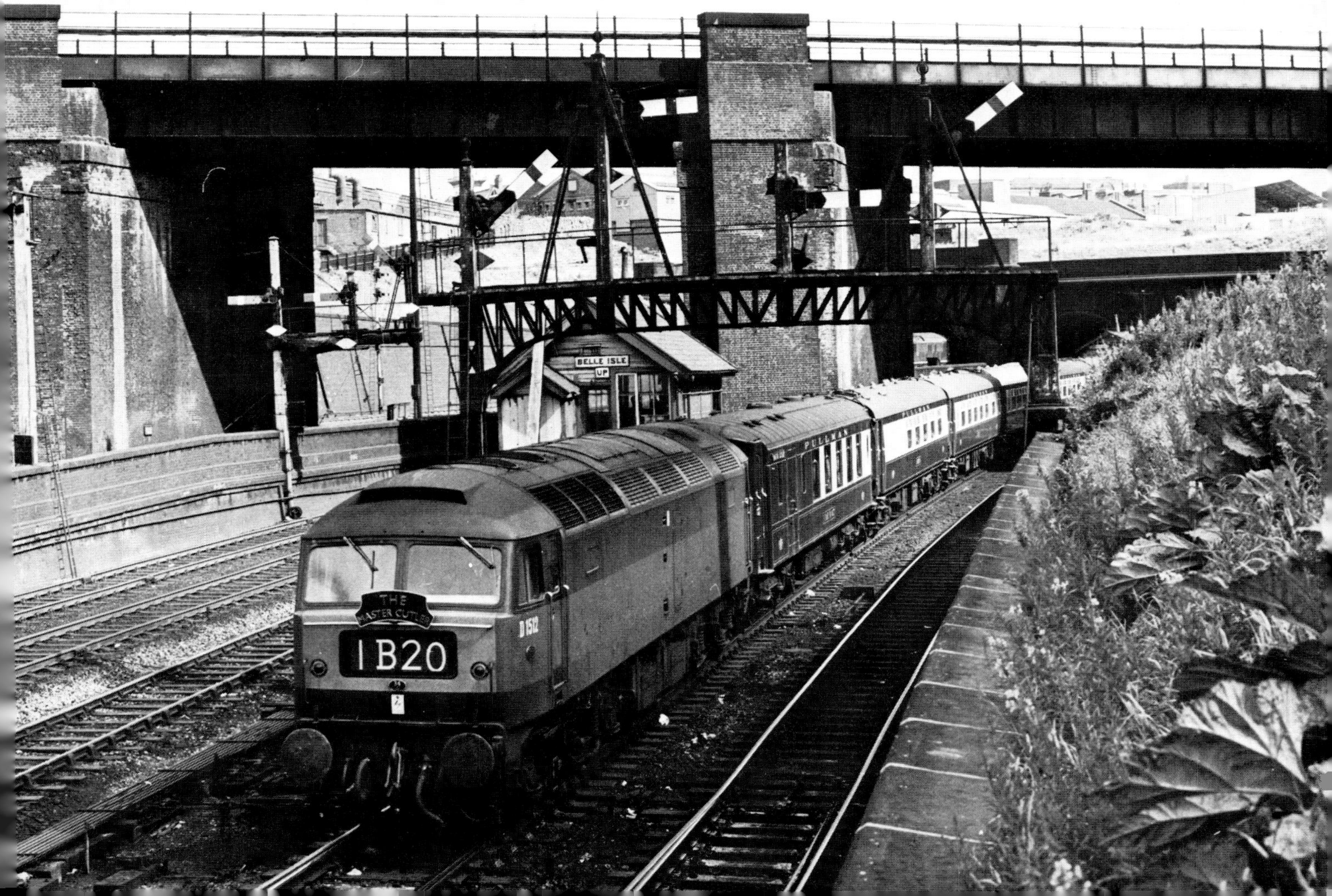
BELLE ISLE
UP
THE MASTER CUTLER
1B20
D1512
PULLMAN

A bit more variety 'twixt the Tunnels.

*Above:* Class N2 0-6-2T No 69548 sweats up the hill with empty stock from Kings Cross, whilst A4 Pacific No 60026 *Miles Beevor* comes off Top Shed to take the 'Norseman' out of Kings Cross.

*Above right:* Two Class 31 Brush Diesels wait at Belle Isle Box, that on the left with empty stock; that on the right, with parcel vans.

*Right:* A4 Pacific No 60013 *Dominion of New Zealand* slips down the hill to the Station, whilst a Class 31 Brush Diesel makes its way to Hertford.

60028
WALTER K. WHIGHAM
YORKSHIRE PULLMAN
60028

60060
60060

You couldn't ask for a better place for locomotive portraiture than at Belle Isle. The engines come off shed clean, they arrange themselves just south of the signal box and wait, simmering, for anything up to ten minutes. Who, with a camera, could ask for more?

*Opposite:* We have two Pacifics waiting for duty with the Pullmans. The A4 No 60028 is *Walter K. Whigham,* and the A3 Pacific No 60060 is *The Tetrarch.*

*Above:* A1 Pacific No 60156 *Great Central* climbs the bank with a train for Newcastle. An A3 can be seen to the left nosing its way through the Arches from the Top Shed.

We have spent long enough between the Tunnels and we must have a look at the Top Shed. Before doing so, here are three more photographs taken in this photogenic territory.

*Below:* The down 'Elizabethan' (A4 Pacific No 60033 *Seagull*) passes A4 Pacific No 60014 *Silver Link* rostered for the down 'Flying Scotsman' from Kings Cross.

*Right:* These engines were called 'Baby Deltics'. None of them now remains in service. Here, No D5901 takes an evening suburban train out of Kings Cross.

*Below right:* A4 Pacific No 60017 *Silver Fox* slips down the hill with the breakfast train from Leeds.

To the west of the main line, and invisible to the passenger who likes shed-spotting, is the Kings Cross Top Shed. During the 1950s, before the diesels invaded Eastern territory, this shed provided lodging for 19 A4s, 8 A1s, and 9 A3s, which gave a stud of 36 Pacifics; that seems a lot, but I would guess that during a busy summer, the Shed Master would find himself short of Pacifics. With all these Pacifics about it was a good place to visit; the best times were between 8am and 9am and between 2.30pm and 3.30pm. Within these hours, locomotives were being prepared for the morning and afternoon traffic to the north from Kings Cross.

The upper picture on the opposite page shows the morning preparations. The three A4s, from left to right, will take the Newcastle, the 'Flying Scotsman', and the non-stop 'Elizabethan'.

The lower picture shows the A4 No 60026 *Miles Beevor* with the cod's mouth open for removal of ash from the smoke box.

*Below:* Three Pacifics on Back Pits at Top Shed.

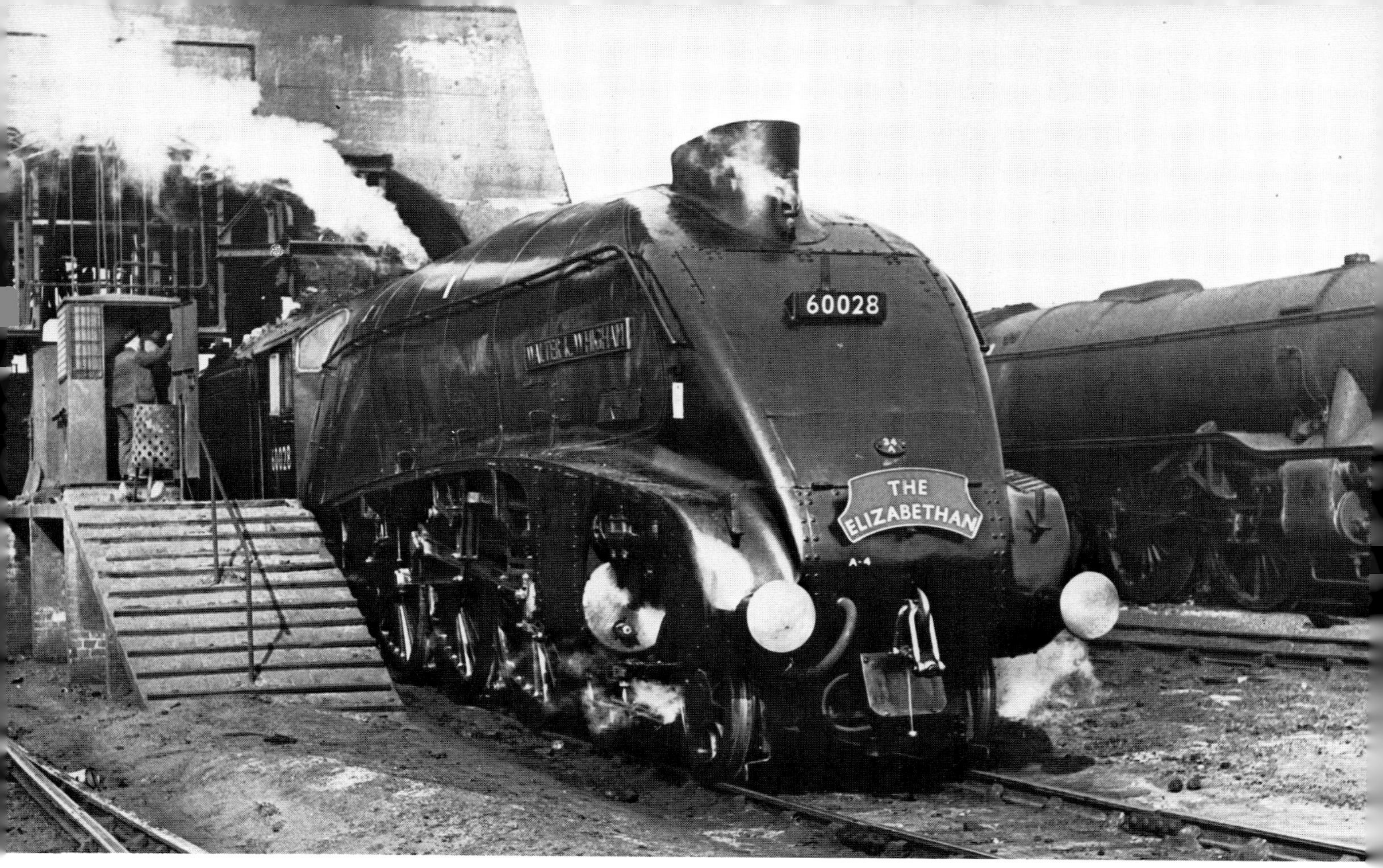
60028
THE ELIZABETHAN

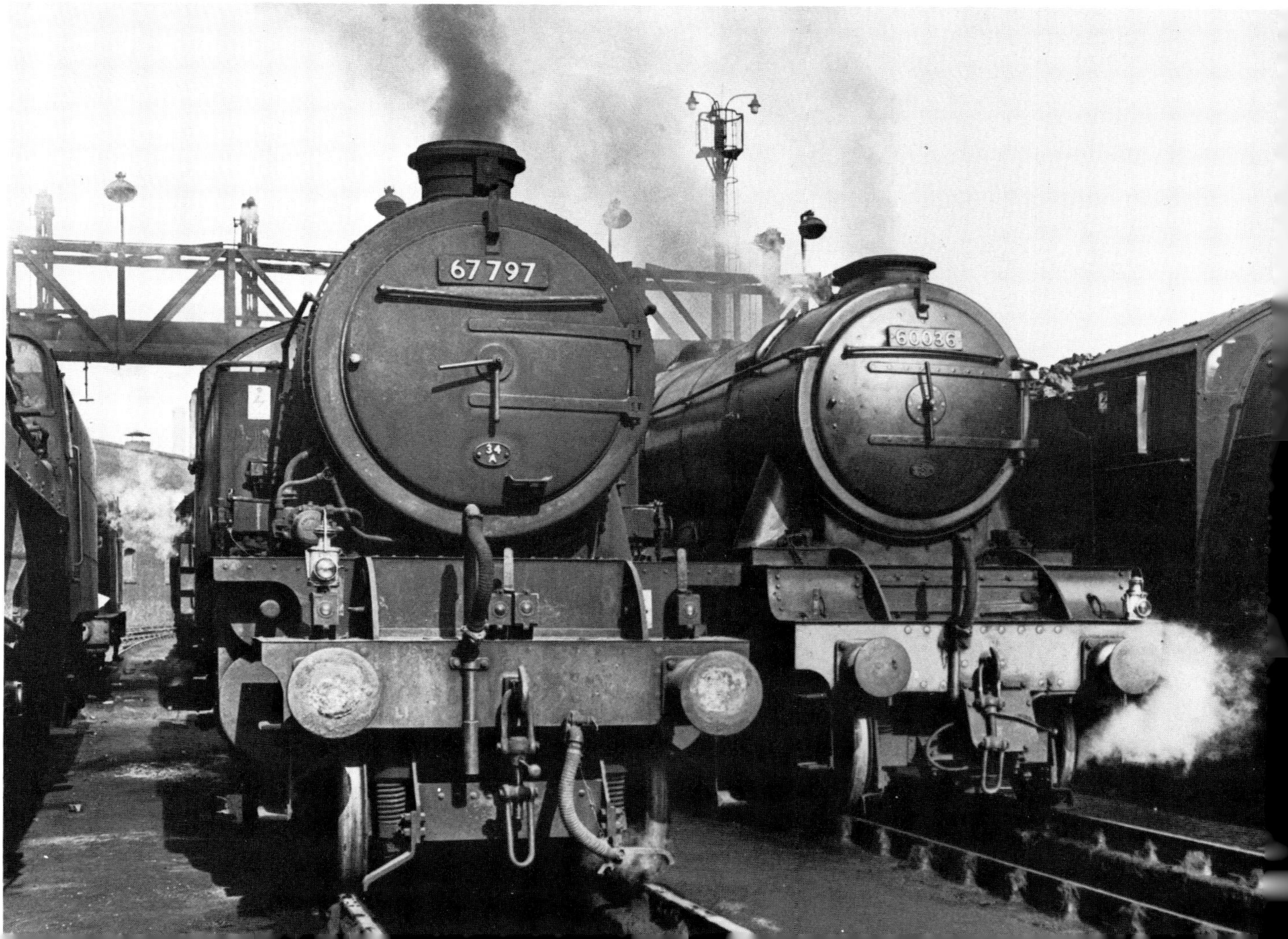
67797
60036

Three more shots at the Top Shed.

*Left:* A4 Pacific No 60028 *Walter K. Whigham* tops up its tender at the coaling stage before setting out for Kings Cross to take the Elizabethan' non-stop to Edinburgh. Note the burnished buffers and the beautiful condition of the engine.

*Below left:* Class V1 2-6-2T No 67797 and A3 Pacific No 60036 *Colombo.* The gantry in the brackground carried the water supply which provided 1000 gallons per minute for locomotive tenders.

*Below:* Morning panorama at Top Shed; picture dominated by grubby V2 No 60914.

My contacts with Kings Cross drivers were frequent, and I found them to have a high level of enthusiasm for their job. It was not often that Kings Cross drivers lost time: they usually made prodigious efforts to regain it. It was a great encouragement to the toplink to have their own engines allocated to them, which was the case up to 1961, when the non-stops were withdrawn.

We are north of Copenhagen tunnel, half way up the hill to Finsbury Park.

*Above:* A3 Pacific No 60105 *Victor Wild* bursts out of the tunnel with train for Leeds and Bradford.

*Above right:* A4 Pacific No 60015 *Quicksilver* moves sedately up the hill with an extra for the West Riding.

*Right:* Breakfast train from Leeds coasts down Holloway Bank. Class 55 Deltic No 9015 *Tulyar.*

60015
364

MACHINE TOOLS
1E02

1A16
D9009

No. 2509

*Left:* Down 'Flying Scotsman' hums up Holloway Bank. Class 55 Deltic No 9009 *Alycidon*

*Below left:* Down Newcastle express passes New Barnet. Class A4 Pacific No 2509 *Silver Link*

*Below:* Class 55 Deltic No 9015, later to be named *Tulyar,* flashes through Hadley Wood Station with down 'Yorkshire Pullman'.

YORKSHIRE PULLMAN
4481

1A14

*Above left:* A3 Pacific No 4481 *St Simon* approaches Potters Bar station with north-bound 'Yorkshire Pullman'.

*Left:* Class 55 Deltic No 9007 *Pinza* approaches Hadley Wood station with express for Edinburgh.

*Above:* Gresley's 4-6-4 locomotive 10000 emerges from Potters Bar Tunnel with a train from London to Newcastle. This engine was a 'one-off'. It was one of Gresley's experiments – a four cylinder compound with a steam pressure of 450psi. Built at Darlington, it made its operational appearance in 1929. No 10000 proved a troublesome engine to maintain, and was, by general consent, not a success.

There is a spaciousness about the railway here since the tracks were quadrupled. The grass embankment is conveniently laid out for the photographer. Although the trains are still climbing, the Deltics are batting along here at speeds up to 80mph.

Here are two Deltics, heading north. On the left, No 9021 *Argyll and Sutherland Highlander* takes a morning train from Kings Cross to the West Riding.

On the right, No 9007 *Pinza* whisks the down 'Yorkshire Pullman' through Hadley Wood station.

I make no excuse for including a number of Deltics amongst these pictures. Since they were introduced on the East Coast Route in 1961 they have given sterling service. The locomotives weigh 102 tons and have a maximum tractive effort of 50,000 lb. They are strong engines and look it. In my view, it is the most handsome diesel-electric locomotive at work on British Rail.

1A90

Nearly 30 years ago we had the excitement of the locomotive exchanges. In the top picture opposite A4 Pacific No 22 *Mallard* heads the 'Atlantic Coast Express' out of Waterloo.

*Left:* Class 55 Deltic No 9007 *Pinza* thunders through Hatfield station with the down Afternoon 'Talisman'.

*Above:* A3 Pacific No 2560 *Pretty Polly* is pictured leaving Potters Bar Tunnel with a train for Newcastle.

CRESCENT JUNCTION
1A46

*Left:* Within an hour of leaving Kings Cross Class 55 Deltic No 9003 *Meld* approaches Peterborough with the afternoon 'Talisman' bound for Edinburgh. As the train passes Crescent Junction Box, it is slowing in order to negotiate the 'dog leg' made by the down fast line through Peterborough station. This was clearly a slack that had to be observed with great care.

*Above:* Class 55 Deltic No 9018, at the time un-named, and later to be *Ballymoss*, leaves Peterborough station with afternoon train for Edinburgh.
Trains now pass Peterborough station at speeds up to 100mph. The fast lines follow the tracks to the right of the picture above. The station has been rebuilt, and the platforms doubled. The picture above shows clearly the nature of the station loop that had to be negotiated by all trains at Peterborough. It always surprised me that they took so long to straighten the track out at Peterborough. From the photograph it would appear to be a simple operation, enabling the non-stops to avoid the platforms as at Darlington.

If you are six feet tall, it is just possible to take photographs of the station at Peterborough from the road bridge. It necessitates standing on tip-toe and resting your arms on a row of spikes. In this uncomfortable position, you are likely to get an agonising attack of cramp at the crucial moment! The two photographs on the opposite page were taken thus, but the situation was made easier by the fact that both trains were stationary.

The upper picture shows Class 37 English Electric locomotive D6744 with a semi-fast for Kings Cross.

*Below left:* Leeds and Bradford train bound for the capital stops briefly at Peterborough. Class 55 Deltic No 9004 *Queens Own Highlander.*

*Below:* A spotless Deltic (No 9015 *Tulyar*) sets out from Peterborough, next stop Kings Cross.

Peterborough is one of the four Cathedral cities through which the East Coast Route passes. The view of Durham Cathedral is the most striking. Peterborough Cathedral and York Minster are not easily seen from the train. Newcastle, with its lantern tower, is easily seen from the High Level Bridge. On a clear day, and if you know exactly where to look, Lincoln Cathedral is visible to the east of the line between Newark and Retford.

Trains stopping at Grantham were confronted with a respectable climb of five miles up to Stoke Summit. Here, under grey skies, A4 Pacific No 60014 *Silver Link* (*above*) sets out from Grantham with an up Newcastle express.

*Above right:* One of the WD 'Austerity' 2-8-0 locomotives, No 90185, climbs to Stoke Summit with a loose-coupled goods train.

*Right:* Grantham Shed, now no more. A1 Pacific No 60124 *Kenilworth*, and Class O2 2-8-0 No 63923.

Grantham, in the days of steam, was a place of considerable interest. Engines and crews were changed here on many of the northbound expresses. Grantham had a stud of Pacifics which took over the Scottish trains from Kings Cross. To avoid lodging turns, which were not popular on the Eastern Region, Grantham crews worked to Newcastle and return.

63923
60124
KENILWORTH

61538

6E
85
D6800

*Above left:* B12 4-6-0 No. 61538 sets out for Nottingham with a train from Grantham. These good-looking engines are a Gresley rebuild of the original Holden G.E. design of 1911.

*Left:* Class 37 English Electric diesel No D6800 emerges from Peascliffe Tunnel north of Grantham with loose coupled freight.

The picture above shows a Peppercorn A1 Pacific, No 60134 *Foxhunter,* starting the climb from Grantham to Stoke with a Leeds-Bradford train. I often rode the footplate of these engines: they were very rarely short of steam but occasionally the engine showed an alarming tendency to 'snake' at speed, perhaps more alarming to the passenger than to the crew, who were accustomed to it. They were fine engines and always on top of the job. It is sad that no member of this class has been preserved.

Grantham, Newark, Retford to Doncaster is scarcely the most exciting bit of railway line in England. The country is flat and uninteresting. Cooling towers and church spires dominate the landscape. The old Great North Road keeps the line company most of the way. From the locomotive point of view, the work is comparatively easy.

*Left:* Class A5 4-6-2T No 69822 sets course for Nottingham out of Grantham.

*Below left:* Class K2 2-6-0 No 61732 heads a freight train near Tuxford.

*Below:* A1 Pacific No 60119 *Patrick Stirling* south of Retford with an express from Leeds to Kings Cross.

And so to Doncaster, the focal point of the old Great Northern.

*Above:* The Up 'Tees-Tyne Pullman' passes the 'Plant' at Doncaster, where so many of the GN and LNER locomotives were built. Class 55 Deltic No 9001 *St Paddy.*

*Above right:* Enter a fitter to bestow his attentions on A1 Pacific No 60149 *Amadis* at Doncaster Shed.

*Right:* Class 49 Brush diesel-electric picks up after stopping at Doncaster station with an express from Newcastle.

60149

1E13

I cannot resist a foray to the west to spend some time on the line from Doncaster to Leeds – strictly speaking, I suppose, not the East Coast Route, but traffic to the old West Riding uses 156 miles of the East Coast Route as far as Doncaster. It diverges to the west just north of Doncaster station and makes for the Cathedral City of Wakefield; there, in the days of steam, trains were divided, the front section proceeding to Leeds with the engine which had brought the train from London, the rear portion, usually in the care of a B1, proceeding to Bradford.

*Below:* A3 Pacific No 60063 *Isinglass* makes a smoky start from Leeds Central for London Kings Cross.

*Right:* Class 55 Deltic No 9007 *Pinza* passes Lofthouse Colliery with breakfast train from West Riding to London.

*Below right:* Evening train from Leeds to London at Copley Hill: A4 Pacific No 60033 *Seagull.* I have to admit that this emission of smoke was by arrangement, as the two heads stuck out of the cab would suggest!

1F07

60033
SEAGULL

*Above:* I think that the word 'hustle' would aptly describe the impression given by A4 Pacific No 60028 *Walter K. Whigham* as it makes for Kings Cross with an afternoon train from Leeds.

*Above left:* A travel-stained A3 Pacific, No 60062 *Minoru,* at Wortley South with an evening train for the Capital.

*Left:* Steam parade at Leeds Central. Left to right: Class N1 0-6-2T No 69483, Class J50 0-6-0T No. 68978, and A3 Pacific No 60055 *Woolwinder*. The Pacific is taking the up 'White Rose' to Kings Cross.

Leeds Central was a somewhat cramped station and had, in consequence, operational problems. From the observer's point of view, this was all to the good, as all the traffic and engine movements were confined to a small area. Therefore you didn't miss much of what was going on.

*Above:* Brush Class 47 Diesel-electric No 1508 passes Copley Hill Carriage Sheds with morning train from Kings Cross to Leeds.

*Above right:* Class 55 Deltic No 9003 *Meld* in Leeds Central station at the end of its run with the breakfast train from Kings Cross.

*Right:* A4 Pacific No 60032 *Gannet* on the curve at Holbeck with the 5.25 pm Leeds Central to Kings Cross.

1N03
60032 
GANNET
60032

586
60096

The line from Leeds Central to Wakefield was a continuous climb from Central Station to Ardsley – up the bank out of Leeds, through the old Holbeck High Level station, past the Copley Hill Sheds, then a breather for half a mile from Wortley South Box, then up the hill again through Beeston and Tingley Tunnel to Ardsley. Some magnificent smoke effects were to be seen as engines tackled this bank.

*Above left:* A3 Pacific No 60096 *Papyrus* at Wortley South with a Bank Holiday extra for London.

*Above:* A4 Pacific No 60025 *Falcon* passes Copley Hill Shed with 9.50am Leeds to London train.

*Left:* The 07.55 hours train from Kings Cross rolls down the hill to Leeds Central: Class 55 Deltic No 9015 *Tulyar.*

The 'Queen of Scots' Pullman diverged from the East Coast Route at Doncaster. It found its way to Leeds Central usually behind an A1 Pacific. At Leeds Central it would lose two of its coaches for Bradford and reverse. A Neville Hill Pacific would follow it down the hill to Leeds Central and couple on for the next stage of the journey to Newcastle, where engines would be changed again. The Pullman would stop at Harrogate after leaving Leeds, and then re-join the East Coast Route at Northallerton.

*Below:* A3 Pacific No 60081 *Shotover* at Wortley Junction with the down 'Queen of Scots' Pullman.

Leeds Central was not a particularly handsome station. It had no frontage on to Wellington Street, only a 'side-age'. It was, in fact, a scruffy station, but over the years I grew very fond of it. I had many friends in A Box at the end of the station. The station is now demolished and there stands on the site an enormous building put up by the Post Office. Central Station, from a railway point of view, was a Leeds Palace of Varieties, so rich was the variety of engines which worked into the station.

*Right:* Class 55 Deltic No 9009 *Alycidon* backs on to train for London.

*Below right:* D0260 *Lion* at Beeston with the up 'Yorkshire Pullman'.

Leeds A Box was a wonderful place for taking photographs, as this picture (*above*) shows. A1 Pacific No 60117 *Bois Roussel* backs on to a train for Kings Cross.

*Above right:* A3 Pacific No 60106 *Flying Fox* on a sharp November day near Elland Road – home of Leeds United, with midday train from Leeds to London.

*Right:* Class 55 Deltic No 9020 *Nimbus* at Hare Park Junction with London train.

Back to the East Coast Route from our visit to Leeds. Where better to re-join it than in the York area? Here we have three freight trains.

*Above:* B16/2 4-6-0 No 61457 at Dringhouses.

*Above right:* O4/1 2-8-0 No 63654 at Holgate. This locomotive is a Robinson Great Central design.

*Right:* Class 4 MT 2-6-0 No 43098 comes off the Selby swing bridge with southbound freight.

63654
43098

The line immediately south of York Station presented wonderful photographic possibilities. In the first place, there was an abundance of traffic, a rich variety of motive power; there was the backcloth of the City of York prominent in which was the Minster; then there was the road bridge at Holgate which gave a wonderful, if irregular, pitch for Treacy and his camera. These three pictures show something of the variety to be expected around York in the 1950s.

*Left:* A 19th century engine at work for British Railways. With a train from York to Doncaster class D20 4-4-0 No 62343 at Holgate. This engine was introduced in 1899 and designed by W. Wordsell.

*Below left:* Neck and neck out of York. A train for Birmingham behind Stanier 2 cyl 4-6-0 No 44811, and a train from Scarborough to Leeds behind Class D49 4-4-0 No 62772 *The Sinnington.* This picture was a wonderful fluke. I have been accused of fixing it, but this was not the case.

*Below:* K3 2-6-0 No 61838 moves off with a train of ash from a power station.

60809

More of the York variety. Nice to see a shapely 'Jubilee' quietly brewing up in York Station. 'Jubilee' 3 cyl 4-6-0 No 45602 *British Honduras* (*above*) waits to leave York with train for Bristol.

*Above left:* Two D49 'Hunt' class 4-4-0s leave York for Leeds with a holiday excursion.

*Left:* An unusually clean V2, No 60809, leaves York with Newcastle to Liverpool train. Next stops Leeds, where the V2 will come off and be replaced by an Edge Hill rebuilt 'Scot'.

8N
Nº 4498

60109

Once, there was a station at Holgate, built to handle the race traffic at York. Now, nothing of the station remains but the platforms, and these are very useful for people with cameras hunting the steam engine rather than picking winners at Knavesmire.

*Above:* B1 4-6-0 No 61337 leaves York with a train for Sheffield.

*Above left:* Under the curving roof of York Station, A4 Pacific No 4493 heads an Enthusiasts' Excursion.

*Left:* A3 Pacific No 60109 *Hermit* heads south at Holgate with a train for Kings Cross.

These photographs are taken on the western approaches to York. Through the station, the line runs briefly from east to west. These trains, all northbound, are running west for about half a mile before swinging north again for the race across the Plain of York to Darlington.

*Below:* A storming start from York by a locomotive bearing a singularly inappropriate name: A3 Pacific No 60071 *Tranquil* with an afternoon train for Newcastle.

*Right:* The 'Flying Scotsman' comes cautiously through York Station: Class 55 Deltic No 9015 *Tulyar.* On the right of the picture is the Royal Station Hotel, which celebrated its Centenary in 1977. From the landing windows there are superb views of the line from the north. The other large building, slightly to the left of the centre, is the headquarters of Eastern Region – a magnificent set of offices, spacious and well-appointed, built by the North Eastern Railway.

*Below right:* V2 No 60975 tops up its tender under the coaling stage at York.

1A16
THE FLYING SCOTSMAN
60975 
60975
BRITISH RAILWAYS
T
V-2

*Above left:* Class 55 Deltic No 9004 *Queens Own Highlander* emerges from York Station with the down 'Flying Scotsman'.

*Left:* A3 Pacific No 60073 *St Gatien* sets out from York with train from East Anglia to Newcastle.

*Above:* A1 Pacific No 60128 *Bongrace* shifts a heavy train out of York, bound for Edinburgh and Glasgow.

York was a good place to be during the lunch hour. Between 1pm and 2.30pm there was an impressive procession in both directions, both 'Flying Scotsmen', trains to and from Bristol, East Anglia, and Liverpool, producing a wide variety of motive power.

There were divided feelings about transferring the National Railway Museum from Clapham to York; I should think that there are few now who do not wholeheartedly accept that this was a change for the better. The two roundhouses at York Shed have been adapted skilfully and imaginatively for the display of locomotives. The two turntables facilitate the movement of the exhibits. There is an excellent gallery which provides a superb view of the exhibition. Here are two photographs of the York Shed – on the left, as it is today with beautifully polished locomotives in the Museum; on the right, as it was in the 1950s – not so clean, but cleaner than most running sheds.

61084
60126

Three more at Leeman Road. The picture below has always been one of my favourites. It shows York Motive Power Depot at midday. There is the smoke-laden atmosphere, men moving about in the haze, and the shafts of light, all so common to a shed in the days of steam. Two V2s, a B16, and two A1s are shown in the picture.

*Right:* Too clean to be real! In the National Railway Museum LBSCR *Gladstone,* LNER V2, No 4771 *Green Arrow*, and LNER A4 No 4468 *Mallard.*

*Below right:* The last steam engine to be built by British Rail. Class 9F 2-10-0 No 92220 *Evening Star* built at Swindon. We were proud, and grateful to the authorities of the Science Museum, to have this locomotive on loan to us at the Keighley & Worth Valley Railway, where it was a great draw. Here it is having attention from Frank Bilton, one of the Museum staff, after an airing on an enthusiasts' trip.

GREEN ARROW
No 4468 
92220
EVENING STAR
92220

*Left:* B16 No 61417 comes off the King Edward VIIth Bridge at Newcastle with parcels train.

*Below left:* V2 No 60979 hustles a freight train between Thirsk and Northallerton.

*Below:* I suppose I ought to ask to be forgiven for including this picture. I do so because it depicts an historic occasion, and a pulpit, the like of which I had never used before.

The date was 17 August 1975, the place, Darlington Bank Top Station, the occasion, a Television Service put out by Tyne-Tees TV to mark the 150th Anniversary of the Stockton & Darlington Railway. The pulpit was the tender of Stephenson's *Locomotion.* What more appropriate? The preacher – Bishop Eric Treacy.

*Reproduced by permission of the Northern Echo.*

60005
A-4
NORTHUMBERLAND

60023
THE FLYING SCOTSMAN
A-4
GATESHEAD

During my days in Yorkshire, time and Eastern Region permitting, I would ride on the footplate of the northbound 'North Briton' from Leeds to Newcastle Central, and return to York on the footplate of the southbound 'Heart of Midlothian'. Going north we would usually have one of Neville Hill's immaculate A3s, and coming back a Haymarket A1. This would give me over five hours' prowling round the neighbourhood of Newcastle Central, and there would be plenty to see. Around midday, there would be the 'Elizabethan', the 'Flying Scotsman', and the Bristol, all southbound; in the early afternoon, the big stuff from the south would rumble over the King Edward VIIth Bridge into Central Station.

*Above left:* Gateshead's A4 No 60005 *Sir Charles Newton,* gets a double yellow as it crosses the KE VII Bridge over the County Boundary.

*Left:* Another Gateshead A4, No 60023 *Golden Eagle* in the suburbs of Gateshead with the up 'Flying Scotsman'.

*Above:* A Class N8 0-6-2 tank engine crosses the King Edward Bridge with a local train, going I know not where.

Southbound Pacifics at Newcastle.

*Above left:* A1 Pacific No 60142 *Edward Fletcher* comes to a standstill with the up 'Heart of Midlothian' and lines up conveniently with V3 2-6-2T No 67636.

*Left:* A3 Pacific No 60080 pulls out of Newcastle Central with train for Bristol.

*Above:* Under what was one of the most impressive and confusing signal gantries in the country, A3 Pacific No 60092 *Fairway* leaves Tyneside for Bristol.

60147
THE
FLYING
SCOTSMAN
60147
60007

It was always a teaser deciding which end of Newcastle station to be in the summer, as there was so much happening at both ends. The ancient Keep in Newcastle also provided a splendid elevated grandstand for viewing proceedings at Newcastle Central.

*Left:* The leaning tower of the local church indicates slight lifting of the camera at the time of exposure. Spotless A1 Pacific No 60147 *North Eastern* sets out from Newcastle Central with the up 'Flying Scotsman'.

*Below left:* You can't see him but Bill Hoole was at the controls of A4 Pacific No 60007 *Sir Nigel Gresley* as it sets out for the south with an express from Edinburgh.

*Below:* An example of the superb lighting conditions in Newcastle Central Station, as A4 Pacific No 60012 *Commonwealth of Australia* backs on to the down 'Flying Scotsman'.

*Below:* Exit the 'North Briton' from Newcastle, behind Gateshead Pacific No 60129 *Guy Mannering.* Alas, the light penetrated my dark slide, hence the rays to the left of the picture. This was a frequent occurrence in the days of plate cameras. Nevertheless, this picture is one that I would wish to include.

*Right:* We travel 67 miles north from Newcastle for this picture. Across Stephenson's magnificent Border Bridge K3 2-6-0 No 61983 eases a freight train into the station loop. The apparently enormous length of this train is explained by the fact that two freight trains are passing each other on the bridge.

*Below right:* A4 Pacific No 60004 *William Whitelaw* at Berwick station with express from Glasgow and Edinburgh to London.

3685

60004

*Above left:* An unidentified K3 2-6-0 near Burnmouth with train of oil tankers.

*Left:* In sight of the sea, A4 Pacific No 60004 *William Whitelaw* sets out on the last stage of its journey to Edinburgh.

*Above:* At almost exactly the same spot on the same day, A3 Pacific the 60083 *Sir Hugo* gets going after the Berwick slack with a fitted freight.

1S32
107

*Above:* Actually crossing the Border. V2 2-6-2 No 60885 passes the Border sign with a fitted freight for Millerhill, Edinburgh.

*Above left:* An unidentified V2 2-6-2 skirts the coast near Burnmouth with train for Newcastle.

*Left:* Class 55 Deltic No 9019 *Royal Highland Fusilier* picks up after stopping at Berwick with express for Edinburgh.

For ten miles north of Berwick, the railway follows the coast line. It leaves the sea at Ayton and rejoins the coast at the village of Cockburnspath. Even on a dull day, there is a remarkable intensity in the light, as the lower picture on the opposite page shows.

Three Diesel-electrics, the numbers of which I cannot trace.

*Above:* A Class 55 Deltic at Grantshouse with the train that used to be the 'Afternoon Talisman', but which has now lost its title. It is the 4pm from Edinburgh Waverley to Kings Cross.

*Above right:* An English Electric Class 40 descends Cockburnspath Bank with train of oil tankers.

*Right:* A Brush class 47 with morning train from Newcastle to Edinburgh.

Perhaps 200yds to the north of Penmanshiel Tunnel is a bridge over the main line, which leads into the woods, and to a crofter's dwelling. It is a splendid place for taking photographs. In the days of steam, trains used to fight their way to the top at about 40mph. Nowadays, the Deltics flash up the hill as if it were not there.

Just over 30 years ago, the cutting between Penmanshiel and Cockburnspath suffered considerable damage from the flood water which cascaded through Penmanshiel Tunnel, bringing about a landslip not far from where the A4 is photographed. On that day in in 1948, it was estimated that 6in of rain fell in 24hr, with the result that small streams became raging torrents sweeping away bridges and track. This was a disaster, the magnitude of which has no parallel in the history of British Railways.

*Above:* The down 'Flying Scotsman' descends Cockburnspath Bank: Class 55 Deltic No 55020 *Nimbus*.

*Above:* The up 'Elizabethan' in the woods at Penmanshiel: A4 Pacific No 60024 *Kingfisher*. The audience consists of Mrs Laidlaw, her son, and their dog. I hope she keeps well. No doubt the dog has passed into whatever existence awaits dead dogs, and the youngster, probably, is married with kids of his own, for the photograph was taken 20 years ago.

62490
62490
60031
A-4

Although the Deltics tear up Cockburnspath Bank with scant respect for the gradient, the steam engines left you in no doubt that they were working hard, and splendid they looked as they battled with the incline.

*Left:* Class D34 4-4-0 No 62490 *Glen Fintaig* ambles up the bank with pick-up goods.

*Below left:* A4 Pacific No 60031 *Golden Plover* approaches Penmanshiel Tunnel with morning train from Glasgow to Kings Cross.

*Below:* At Portobello East Junction: A4 Pacific No 60027 *Merlin* with London express.

1A14
DP2

In the Edinburgh suburbs. At Portobello, the Waverley Route for Carlisle via Hawick diverged from the East Coast Route. The Waverley Route, alas, is no more.

*Above left:* V3 2-6-2T No 67668 brings a train of empty stock to Craigentinny.

*Left:* English Electric experimental locomotive No DP2 takes the Summer relief 'Flying Scotsman' through Craigentinny to Edinburgh.

*Above:* Five minutes after noon, A3 Pacific No 60068 *Sir Visto* leaves Edinburgh Waverley with train for Carlise via the Waverley Route.

60160
N
60160

I feel about Edinburgh as I feel about no other city in Britain. It possesses a majesty and style that I find unique. Its shops are good, if expensive, it's cafés welcoming, and there is always the Castle keeping a watchful eye on what is going on. Princes Street as a whole is impressive, but taken building by building, pretty awful. You will hear every accent and language in the world along Princes Street in the summer. Right in the heart of Edinburgh is Waverley station, and amongst all the sounds of the city, none is more frequently heard than the rumble of trains as they thread Princes Street Gardens. Fifteen years ago, you would have heard the chime of an A4 on its way to, or from, Haymarket Sheds: now, all you hear is the hooter of a diesel, My experience of railwaymen in the Edinburgh area is that they are a nice lot, welcoming and helpful. I have, therefore, always enjoyed my visits to Edinburgh Waverley. It is a station at which there is never a dull moment. Here are two shots at Waverley. On the left, the departure of the 10 o'clock 'Flying Scotsman': A1 Pacific No 60160 *Auld Reekie*. On the right, the arrival of the non-stop 'Elizabethan' from Kings Cross behind A4 Pacific No 60027 *Merlin.*

THE
ELIZABETHAN
1A33
D9021

60012
THE
ELIZABETHAN
60012

Morning at Waverley. The Deltics took over from the A4s with the 'Elizabethan', no longer non-stop as the train halted at Newcastle to change crews, there being no corridor connection with the train on the Deltics.

*Left:* The 'Elizabethan' gets away to London behind un-named Deltic No 9021.

*Below left:* The 'Elizabethan' steam-hauled by A4 Pacific No 60012 *Commonwealth of Australia.*

Haymaket Shed always turned out a sparkling locomotive for the 'Queen of Scots' Pullman. The Edinburgh engine worked the train to Newcastle, where it was taken forward by a Neville Hill engine to Leeds, usually an A3 which had brought the 'North Briton' from Leeds to Newcastle in the morning.

*Below:* A4 Pacific No 60011 *Empire of India* leaves Waverley Station with the up Pullman.

The east end of Waverley Station was well laid out for photographic purposes, as these pictures show. The massive clock tower of the North British Hotel dominates the background. Here are two photographs of the same train with differing Motive Power. It is the 11 o'clock from Glasgow to London on the left, the train leaves behind un-named Deltic No 9010; on the right, the train sets out behind A4 Pacific No 60010 *Dominion of Canada.*

60010

*Below:* With a good deal of extraneous steam, A1 Pacific No 60142 *Edward Fletcher* takes the up 'Flying Scotsman' out of Waverley station.

*Below right:* A Deltic hums gently at the head of the up 'Heart of Midlothian' in Waverley station.

*Right:* Class 55 Deltic No 9009 *Alycidon* on the up 'Flying Scotsman' is joined by English Electric Class 40 No 286.

THE
FLYING
SCOTSMAN
D9009
E202

*Above:* The down 'Flying Scotsman' arrives at Waverley station slightly before time. The locomotive is Deltic No 9021 *Argyll and Sutherland Highlander.*

*Above right:* Class 25/2 D7591 at west end of Waverley station with train from Dundee.

*Right:* A2 Pacific No 60537 *Bachellor's Button* leaves Haymarket Shed for duty at Edinburgh Waverley.

End of the line – two views at Haymarket Shed.

*Above:* A4 Pacific No 60009 *Union of South Africa* returns to its home shed having brought the Elizabethan from London.

*Below:* A2 Pacific No 60538 *Velocity*, B1 4-6-0 No 61322 and A3 Pacific No 60099 *Call Boy*, at rest at Haymarket.